SAINSBURY'S

Ba[illegible]

40 original recipes with a complete guide to successful barbecuing

Jim Marks

Contents

Published exclusively for J Sainsbury plc
Stamford House Stamford Street
London SE1 9LL
by Martin Books
Simon & Schuster Consumer Group
Grafton House 64 Maids Causeway
Cambridge CB5 8DD

Published 1995
ISBN 0 85941 876 6

Printed and bound in the UK by Bath Press Colourbooks
Design: Green Moore Lowenhoff
Photography: Iain Bagwell
Styling: Rachel Jukes
Food preparation: Berit Vinegrad
Typesetting: Goodfellow & Egan Ltd, Cambridge

Pictured on the front cover: Cranberry Glazed Chicken Wings (page 48)

Introduction

Barbecuing has gained enormous popularity in Britain as an ideal way both to entertain friends and to cater for everyday family meals. A barbecue should provide at least as much fun and enjoyment for the cook as for the guests. It should be a completely relaxing experience for everyone.

I have set out to explain some of the more practical aspects of barbecuing in order to show just how simple outdoor cooking can be and, I hope, to encourage some readers to be a little more adventurous than usual. So in addition to the perennial favourites, such as hamburgers and garlic bread, I trust some will be persuaded to try their hand at smoke-cooking, baking and stir-frying.

Happy barbecuing!

Jim Marks

BARBECUE BASICS

Selecting your barbecue The choices of barbecues today is overwhelming in its range and diversity, so before you look at any models, try to have a clear idea of the ideal barbecue for your normal catering requirements. You probably have seen or used barbecues that are fuelled by charcoal, gas or electricity – your choice of barbecues will narrow considerably if you decide ahead which type of fuel best serves your needs.

Charcoal-burning barbecues Portable barbecues are ideal for family picnics. To be truly portable a barbecue should measure no more than 40 cm (16 inches) in diameter. This small size will handle eight or more burgers or steaks at a time.

Disposable barbecues have a basic grill over a shallow tray containing 'instant-lighting' charcoal, ready for cooking just 15 minutes after lighting. Disposable barbecues can be recycled at least once by refuelling with a small bag of instant-lighting charcoal.

Brazier barbecues are probably the most popular type of barbecue. They are ideal for home use and are available in both rectangular and circular shapes.

Covered barbecues allow you to roast, bake (page 8), and smoke-cook (page 9). They have adjustable air vents that create a through-draught, making them easy to light and allowing good temperature control during cooking. Both square and rectangular units are available, but the distinctive cherry-shaped 'Kettle' model is the most popular.

DIY built-in barbecues are available in kit form. The basic kit should include a chrome-plated grill, ash pan and support brackets along with instructions on how to build the supporting brick or stone structure. Some kits will contain a protective lid or a spit-roast assembly.

Gas barbecues Food cooked on a gas barbecue tastes, smells and looks just as good as food that has been charcoal-grilled: as the juices drip down on to the coals they produce aromatic smoke and it is this that gives the food its magical 'barbecue' flavour and appearance. Both gas and charcoal produce radiant heat, and so are equally effective in generating the necessary barbecue smoke. Gas barbecues use natural lava rock, ceramic briquettes or ceramic-coated metal plates, all of which should last for several years. Gas barbecues are very economical to use, easy to light and extinguish, quick to heat up, allow maximum temperature control and are, to some extent, self-cleaning.

Portable gas barbecues are basic. The lightweight units are powered by small disposable gas cartridges, which can provide up to 1 hour of cooking time and are good for grilling flat foods such as steaks, burgers, fish etc. Larger portable models operate off refillable butane gas cylinders that are much more economical than the disposable cartridges. They are too heavy for casual transport and are more suitable for caravanners, boaters or small-scale cook-outs. Some larger portable barbecues can roast a small chicken or joint, providing the lid is deep enough.

Wagon gas barbecues vary greatly in size, power, cooking capacity and attachments. Some operate off natural gas. The majority have two individually controlled burners that allow you a very accurate control over the cooking temperatures, and they all can be moved fairly easily over short distances. Several models come with rôtisseries and some with a side-burner.

Permanent (built-in) barbecues are basically Wagon-style barbecues minus their undercarriage. They usually have twin burners. Models operating off natural gas are available.

Electric barbecues These are easy and convenient to use with relatively little energy consumption. Electric barbecues give off radiant heat which can grill flat foods or, in some instances, spit-roast a small joint. Heat control is via an adjustable thermostat.

Barbecue checkpoints

- Make sure that any barbecue you use is stable and capable of supporting both food and fuel. If it wobbles, check the assembly before blaming it on poor design.
- If it is a brazier barbecue, does it have a windshield?
- Can you adjust the food grill(s) up and down with ease (try to visualise the grill laden with food) and is the barbecue set up at a comfortable working height?
- Check that the bars of the food grill have an even coating of nickel chrome plating and are spaced closely enough to prevent food from falling through.
- Make certain there are no sharp edges to the barbecue's fire bowl or lid.
- If there is a lid, does it fit neatly and do its air vents adjust easily?
- If you're buying a gas barbecue, make sure that it is 'CE' certified for safety and

performance. Check also that the gas regulator is approved. Electric barbecues should have BEAB approval.

• Again for gas barbecues, check that sufficient lava rock is provided to cover the fire grate in a single crowded layer. Large gaps between the rocks or briquettes may cause flare-ups when fat drips directly on to the burner. Refill packs of lava rock are available.

Barbecue accessories There are many accessories available which make barbecuing that bit easier or more interesting.

• Tongs should have long handles that are easy to manipulate. Avoid those with sharp teeth or jaws which misalign.

• Gloves should be elbow length and made from a thick non-flammable fabric.

• A heavy apron (cotton or cotton mix is best) will protect you from splashes of hot fat.

• Forks should be long-handled with a comfortable grip.

• Basting brushes should be made from natural fibres and the handles long. It is good to have one for applying sauces and a second for oil and fat.

• Wire broilers are available in many shapes and sizes. Fish broilers are the most useful. Long-handled rectangular broilers with closely-spaced wires are ideal for chicken wings.

• Skewers should ideally be flat-bladed, about 5 mm (¼ inch) wide for chunky kebabs. Hardwood or bamboo skewers are good for satay while double-pronged skewers work best for large pieces of food.

• Cleaning brushes should have coarse wire bristles, although I prefer to simply rub over the bars when they are still warm with a crumpled-up ball of aluminium foil (remember to protect your hand for this operation). Alternatively use a liquid barbecue cleaner when cold.

• A food thermometer is useful for checking the internal temperature of meat.

Fuel Charcoal is available as pressed briquettes or as natural lumpwood. The briquettes burn for longer than the lumpwood but are not as easy to light. Both should be made with a high percentage of dense hardwood, such as oak, beech, birch and hickory.

Simpler still are the bags of instant-light charcoal which are widely available. To use, light the corners of the bag and the barbecue will be ready for cooking in about 15 minutes.

Firelighters Warning! Never use petrol, methylated spirits, lighter fluid, naphtha or similar volatile liquids to ignite charcoal. Never add lighting fluid of any kind to any charcoal which has already ignited. If you wish to rekindle the fire, use a solid firelighter. If in doubt that the charcoal is burning, it is safer to start again from scratch.

• Solid firelighters are usually more effective than liquids. They can be based on kerosene or wax. Kerosene has a characteristic odour and produces some smoke while burning. The other types are virtually smokeless and odourless. In every case make sure that the firelighter has completely burnt away before starting to cook.

• Commercial liquid firelighters are non-volatile but shouldn't be added to a lit fire.

• Liquid paste (or jellied kerosene) firelighters are packaged in tubes, making them convenient for picnic barbecues.

• Gas torches operate off a small cartridge of butane gas and are great for lighting fires in windy conditions.

• Electric starters are electrical elements attached to long handles – also good for lighting fires in windy conditions.

• Charcoal chimneys look like giant sugar sifters and use sheets of newspapers to ignite charcoal. They are particularly effective when used with lumpwood charcoal.

Preparing the barbecue To gauge how much fuel is needed, roughly duplicate the food-laden area of the grill with a single layer of charcoal, leaving a small space between each piece.

Build a pyramid-shaped pile of charcoal in the centre of the grate or bowl. Add the firelighter according to the manufacturer's instructions and allow to burn for 15–30 minutes or until most of the coals are covered in grey ash. Spread the coals in a single layer and leave to burn for 5–10 minutes before cooking. First-time barbecuers are advised to allow an extra 20–30 minutes to the time suggested by the charcoal manufacturer.

For spit roasting: build the pyramid of coals towards the rear of the grate or bowl. Add the firelighter and allow to burn for 30–40 minutes or until most of the coals are covered in grey ash.

For roasting and baking: position a drip pan in the centre of the fire grate. Pile an equal amount of charcoal on each side of the pan, add the firelighter and continue as described above. For a cooler temperature, put the drip pan to one side of the grate and pile the charcoal next to it.

Most barbecue food is best cooked at a medium-hot temperature. To judge how hot the fire is, wait until at least 80% of the charcoal has been covered by a greyish ash, then hold your hand, palm down, an inch or two over the food grill. Count the seconds before the heat forces your hand away. If you can hold it there for more than 4 seconds, the temperature is too low for grilling. Roughly speaking, 4 seconds indicates a medium heat, 3 seconds medium-hot and 2 seconds means that the coals are hot. There are several ways to control the cooking temperature, including simply raising the food grill to lower the temperature and vice versa. Widening the spaces between the coals will also lower the cooking temperature while piling them closer together will give off more heat. You can also open the air vents in the fire bowl to increase the through-draught and raise the temperature – or partially close them to lessen the heat.

After cooking put out the fire or allow it to burn out but do not leave a hot barbecue unattended. Use sand to extinguish the fire. Never pour water over the coals while they are in the fire grate as this can damage the barbecue. If using a covered barbecue, simply close the vents

and lid – the fire should be out within half an hour or so.

Safety first

• Burning charcoal emits carbon monoxide, so never light or use your barbecue in a confined space.

• Mount the barbecue on a flat non-slip surface well away from dry shrubbery and wooden fences and sheds.

• Never leave the barbecue unattended when there are children present.

• Avoid flare-ups by using good quality meats (particularly burgers and sausages which can be quite fatty), keeping the fire temperature at a sensible level and by not overloading the grill. Wipe the underside of the barbecue lid occasionally with kitchen paper while the lid is warm to prevent grease from building up. If a flare-up does occur, quickly push the food away from the seat of the flame which should burn itself out in a few seconds.

• Make sure that hot coals are fully extinguished before leaving the barbecue site.

• For evening barbecues make sure the cooking area is well-lit, and that the drinks table is sited well clear of the barbecue.

Food safety Food poisoning bacteria can be found almost everywhere; the following are simple guidelines that should minimise the risk of food poisoning.

• Raw foods and cooked foods must be kept separate. Don't use the same cooking utensils, work surfaces or even aprons for preparing raw food and for barbecuing. If possible, buy two sets of tongs, brushes and chopping boards. Try to vary their colours, shapes and sizes for easy identification.

• Do not baste the food with the same marinade in which it was steeped in its raw state. The marinade should be divided into two batches – one for marinating and the other for basting.

• Thaw frozen poultry in a cool room or in a refrigerator. Allow sufficient time for the poultry to defrost before cooking. A bird will be ready for cooking when its body is pliable, its legs move freely in their joints and the body cavity is completely clear of ice crystals. Once thawed, keep poultry in the refrigerator and cook within 24 hours.

• When thawing frozen poultry or meat, ensure that the thawed juices do not escape on to work surfaces or, in the refrigerator, drip on to other food. Any work surfaces that the juices touch should be thoroughly cleaned.

• Turn all foods over regularly to ensure even cooking.

• When cooking meat and poultry place larger, thicker portions on the barbecue first, away from the most intense heat to ensure thorough cooking without burning.

• Make sure that all food is cooked through, especially poultry, burgers and sausages. When poultry is pierced with a fork or skewer the juices should run clear and not pink. Burgers, or similar products, should be cooked through until the centre is piping hot and no pink colour remains.

Barbecue cooking techniques Grilling is a popular technique for foods which can be

cooked within 30–40 minutes, such as chops, steaks, burgers, fish and shellfish, chicken portions, kebabs and vegetables.

- Marinate food to achieve extra tenderness and/or flavour.
- Ensure fire temperature is adequate before starting to cook.
- To prevent sticking, brush the food grill, skewers, broilers and food with oil before cooking.
- If possible, adjust the food grill to 5–8 cm (2–3 inches) above the fire-bed and sear meat before raising the grill to 10–15 cm (4–6 inches) for the remainder of grilling time. For gas barbecues, simply adjust the temperature setting from high to medium-low.
- To avoid charring or burning the food, apply basting sauces or glazes (particularly those containing sugar) during the final few minutes of grilling.
- Use tongs to turn flat meats rather than the prongs of a fork which could pierce the meat and allow precious juices to escape.
- For even cooking, make up kebabs with foods that have a similar cooking time or part-cook the slower-cooking foods before grilling.
- Before grilling fatty meats such as spare-ribs or pork cutlets, seal them in a foil packet with two tablespoons of water and heat in a moderate oven (or covered barbecue) for about 45 minutes. This will render out a lot of the fat, reducing both the cooking time and the possibility of a flare-up.

Spit-roasting

- Prepare the barbecue (page 6) and check the temperature before cooking.
- Make sure that the food is evenly balanced on the spit-rod and held securely by the tines.
- Poultry and game should be trussed, and protruding wing tips and bones covered with foil to prevent charring.
- When impaling small pieces of meat on a spit, leave a small gap between them so that the heat reaches all surfaces. Make sure that the fire-bed is long enough to cook the meat evenly.
- Unless it is marinated, the joint should be brushed with oil after being mounted on the spit.
- If the drip pan is flush with the fire-bed, fill the pan three-quarters full with water and/or beer or wine. You can then use the flavoured drippings as a savoury baste, perhaps adding herbs to taste.

Roasting and baking

- Prepare the barbecue (page 6) and check the temperature before cooking.
- Position the food directly over the pan and shut the barbecue lid making sure that its air vents are fully open.
- If using a gas barbecue with two burners, position the drip pan to one side under the food grill (the pan should be large enough to catch the drippings from the food but shouldn't encroach into the other side of the barbecue). With the lid open, ignite the gas burner (set on high) opposite to the drip pan. Close the lid and let heat for 5–10 minutes. Position the

food on the grill over the unlit burner and adjust the temperature. Most roasting and baking will require a medium heat.

• When roasting a joint, place packages of foil-wrapped, prepared vegetables around the roast 10–20 minutes before the meat is ready. Carrots should be parboiled first.

• Use a rib rack to increase the barbecue's capacity and make basting easier.

Smoke-cooking Not to be confused with smoking, which 'cures' meats at very low temperatures, smoke-cooking is a 'hot' smoking process which imparts a rich colour and tangy, piquant flavour to roasted foods by applying damp aromatic wood chips to the fire-bed. Smoke-cooking can be achieved using any covered barbecue, charcoal or gas fired, without diverting from the usual temperatures or cooking times. The most popular of smoking woods is hickory but also worth trying are oak, mesquite, cherry, beech, alder, sycamore, poplar and vine – do not use pine or resinous softwoods. Try smoking poultry, pork, lamb, venison, ham, kidneys, sausages and a wide variety of fish, including salmon, trout and mackerel. Eels and oysters are also very suitable for smoke-cooking.

• Scattering a handful of soaked wood chips over the fire-bed roughly half-way through roasting a 1.5 kg (3 lb) chicken should give the skin an attractive mahogany colour with a delicate smoky flavour. The greater the quantity and the earlier you add the wood, the darker the hue and more intense the flavour will be.

• Brushing a glaze over the meat 10–15 minutes before it has finished cooking will add a rich lustre and colour to the skin.

• Place an open pot of baked beans next to the meat during smoke-cooking to give the beans a delicious smoky flavour. Stir the pot occasionally to prevent too crunchy a skin from forming.

RECIPE NOTES

All recipes in this book give ingredients in both metric (g, ml, etc.) and imperial (oz, pints, etc.) measures. Use either set of quantities, but not a mixture of both, in any one recipe.

All teaspoons and tablespoons are level, unless otherwise stated. 1 teaspoon = a 5 ml spoon; 1 tablespoon = a 15 ml spoon.

Egg size is medium (size 3), unless otherwise stated.

Vegetables and fruit are medium-size unless otherwise stated.

Freshly ground black pepper should be used throughout.

PREPARATION AND COOKING TIMES

Preparation and cooking times are included at the head of the recipes as a general guide; preparation times, especially, are approximate and timings are usually rounded to the nearest 5 minutes.

Preparation times include the time taken to prepare ingredients in the list, but not to make any 'basic' recipe.

The cooking times given at the heads of the recipes denote cooking periods when the dish can be left largely unattended, e.g. baking, and not the total amount of cooking for the recipe. Always read and follow the timings given for the steps of the recipe in the method.

Marinades, Bastes, Sauces and Glazes

Marinade is a French term describing a seasoned liquid in which raw meat or fish is steeped before being cooked, in order to enhance its flavour. Marinades might include oil, wine vinegar, fruit juice, cider, beer, herbs and spices or vegetables. The acidic liquid acts as a tenderising agent while the oil helps to moisten very lean meat and prevent it from losing too much of its natural succulence when cooked over a high heat.

The easiest way to marinate smaller cuts of meat is to place them with the marinade in a strong plastic bag, tightly sealed, so that it can be turned frequently. Marinating times vary from 1 hour to several days: generally speaking, the lighter the meat or fish the less time it needs to marinate. If a marinade is applied to the food just before cooking, or during the early stages, it is called a baste. The distinction between a marinade and a sauce can be quite hazy, but usually a sauce is either served as an accompaniment or, if enriched with jam or sugar, brushed on to food during the final 10–15 minutes of cooking to produce an attractive glaze.

Salsa Mexicana

Preparation time: 20 minutes + 30 minutes standing.
Freezing: not recommended. Makes 750 ml (1¼ pints).

Salsa is Spanish for sauce, and the chilli peppers in this hot and spicy salsa give it its name. Try it alongside barbecued steaks and spare-ribs. This can keep for up to 1 week in the refrigerator.

- 2 fresh hot chilli peppers, de-seeded and chopped finely
- 2 onions, chopped finely
- 6 garlic cloves, chopped finely
- 6 firm, ripe tomatoes, skinned, de-seeded and chopped coarsely
- 40 g (1½ oz) fresh coriander leaves, chopped coarsely
- a large pinch of coarse salt
- juice of 3 limes
- 4 tablespoons olive oil

❶ Combine the chilli peppers, onions, garlic, tomatoes and coriander in a large bowl.

❷ Add the salt and stir in the lime juice.

❸ Stir in the olive oil, check the mixture for taste and add more salt if desired.

❹ Cover the bowl and leave the salsa to stand for about 30 minutes to allow the flavours to blend.

Teriyaki Marinade

Preparation time: 5 minutes.
Freezing: recommended. Makes 125 ml (4 fl oz).

Teriyaki is probably the most useful sauce/marinade for the barbecue cook. It has a rich, salty but sweet flavour that is absolutely ideal for marinating, basting, or seasoning chicken portions, pork chops, steaks, kebabs, ribs, salmon and shellfish. This recipe makes enough to marinate about 1.25–1.75 kg (3–4 lb) of meat and will keep for up to 2 months in the refrigerator.

1½ tablespoons clear honey or 2 tablespoons brown sugar
1½ tablespoons sunflower oil
4 tablespoons soy sauce
1 tablespoon dry red wine or red wine vinegar
1 teaspoon grated fresh root ginger or ½ teaspoon freeze-dried ginger
1 garlic clove, crushed

❶ Combine all the ingredients.
❷ Place the food and marinade in a strong, tightly-sealed plastic bag and set in a shallow dish. Refrigerate, turning the bag occasionally. To achieve the best flavour, marinate fish for 2–4 hours, chicken and spare-ribs for at least 4–8 hours and beef for 6–8 hours or longer.

S.O.S. Marinade (Sherry-Orange-Soy)

Preparation time: 5 minutes.
Freezing: recommended. Makes 375 ml (12 fl oz).

An excellent all-round marinade for beef and pork steaks, lamb cutlets and chops, chicken portions, fish and shellfish. This recipe makes enough to marinate 3–4.25 kg (7–10 lb) and can be kept for 1 week in the refrigerator.

3 tablespoons dry sherry
150 ml (¼ pint) orange juice
150 ml (¼ pint) soy sauce
1 tablespoon grated fresh root ginger or 1 teaspoon freeze-dried ginger
4 garlic cloves, crushed

❶ Combine all the ingredients.
❷ Place meat and marinade in a strong, tightly-sealed plastic bag and set into a shallow dish. Refrigerate for 6 hours or overnight.

Sweet and Sour Basting Sauce

Preparation time: 5 minutes.
Freezing: recommended. Makes 400 ml (14 fl oz).

An excellent baste for poultry, pork, ribs and fish steaks and particularly well-suited for a joint of lamb.

300 ml (½ pint) orange juice
4 tablespoons dry white wine
2 tablespoons clear honey
1 tablespoon soy sauce
1 teaspoon mustard powder
¼ teaspoon garlic salt
1 tablespoon brown sugar
salt and pepper

❶ Combine all the ingredients.
❷ Brush the basting mixture over the meat or fish at the beginning of cooking and repeat as the recipe requires.
❸ Heat the remaining baste, stirring, until piping hot. Serve as an accompanying sauce.

Indonesian Satay Sauce

Preparation time: 25 minutes.
Freezing: recommended. Makes 400 ml (14 fl oz).

This spicy and 'mildly' hot sauce can be served hot or cold. Try it with grilled steaks or chicken portions. Add a little more chilli powder or a few drops of Tabasco sauce if you like it even spicier.

2 tablespoons sunflower oil
1 onion, chopped finely
300 ml (½ pint) tomato ketchup
1 tablespoon Worcestershire sauce
2 tablespoons smooth peanut butter
1 tablespoon red wine vinegar
1 garlic clove, crushed
½ teaspoon chilli powder
salt and pepper

❶ Heat the oil in a large heavy-based saucepan. Add the onion and cook until softened.
❷ Add the remaining ingredients and bring the mixture to a boil, stirring constantly. Lower the heat and simmer for 15–20 minutes, stirring occasionally.
❸ Use to baste the food during the final 10 minutes of cooking or serve as a dipping sauce.

Apricot and Rosemary Glaze

Preparation time: 10 minutes.
Freezing: recommended. Makes 300 ml (½ pint).

A tasty and attractive glaze which goes well with poultry, pork and lamb.

500 g (1 lb) apricot jam
1 tablespoon red or white wine vinegar
½ teaspoon crushed rosemary
1 garlic clove, crushed
1 teaspoon Dijon mustard
salt and pepper

❶ Combine all the ingredients in a saucepan and heat, stirring constantly, until the jam has become thin and runny.

❷ Brush the glaze over the meat two or three times during the last 15 minutes or so of cooking.

Hot and Spicy Barbecue Sauce

Preparation time: 10 minutes + 20 minutes standing.
Freezing: recommended. Makes 750 ml (1¼ pints).

The blend of chilli, Tabasco and Worcestershire sauces make this hot enough for even the bravest of barbecuers. The tomato, mustard and honey give this sauce a sweet, spicy edge. It goes well with steaks, hamburgers and chicken portions. Or you can use it as a marinade, in which case this recipe will be sufficient for 6–8 kg (14–18 lb) of meat. It will keep for up to 4 weeks in the refrigerator.

300 ml (½ pint) chilli sauce
300 ml (½ pint) tomato ketchup
3 tablespoons wine vinegar
3 tablespoons tarragon vinegar
3 tablespoons Worcestershire sauce
90 ml (3 fl oz) water
4 tablespoons clear honey
2 dashes of Tabasco sauce
1 teaspoon chilli powder
1 teaspoon mustard powder
½ teaspoon pepper
1 teaspoon salt

❶ Mix all the ingredients together. Add a little more water if the sauce is too thick.

❷ Allow the sauce to stand for about 20 minutes before use.

Fish

Fish benefits enormously from being grilled over a medium-hot heat as this brings out its natural flavour – a flavour enhanced by the smoke created when the juices fall on to the fire-bed below. Shellfish are particularly well-suited to barbecue grilling. Their shells protect against the drying effect of the heat, keeping them succulent and tender.

Tips and techniques for barbecuing fish:

- **Calculate the grilling time of your fish by measuring its thickest part – not its weight. Allow 10 minutes for each 2.5 cm (1 inch) of fish. Do not overcook as the fish will become tough and dry. Shellfish require only minimum grilling. When the meat looks opaque it is ready.**
- **Liberally oil both the grill bars and the side of the fish to be cooked first just before placing the fish on the grill. If using a broiler, coat the inside surface of the basket as well as the fish and the grill bars just before placing the broiler on the heat.**
- **Placing whole fish across the grill bars will reduce the possibility of the skin sticking to the grill.**

Garlic and Mustard Grilled Prawns

Preparation time: 30 minutes + 5–6 hours marinating + 5–8 minutes cooking.
Freezing: not recommended. Serves 4–6.

One of those messy-but-nice dishes!

1 kg (2 lb) large uncooked tiger prawns
125 ml (4 fl oz) olive or groundnut oil
3 tablespoons lemon juice
1 onion, chopped finely
3 garlic cloves, chopped
25 g (1 oz) parsley, chopped finely
1 teaspoon mustard powder
1 teaspoon salt

❶ Prepare the prawns by pulling the legs off, leaving the shells and tails intact. Carefully snip the shells open along the back of the prawns. Cut gently into the meat using the tip of your knife to hook out the dark vein. Rinse the prawns under cold running water.

❷ Combine the remaining ingredients in a bowl and mix thoroughly. Add the prawns and turn to coat well with the mixture. Cover the bowl with clingfilm or foil and refrigerate for 5–6 hours.

❸ Prepare and pre-heat the barbecue for grilling (page 6).

❹ Drain the prawns and thread on to wet bamboo or wooden skewers.

❺ Grill the prawns over medium-high heat, basting frequently with the remaining marinade, for 2–4 minutes on each side until they just change colour. Do not overcook as they will become tough.

Spicy Lime Sardines

Preparation time: 15 minutes + 1 hour standing + 6–8 minutes cooking.
Freezing: not recommended. Serves 4.

Try serving these sardines on crusty bread, allowing the juices from the fish to soak in for a minute or two before eating.

8 fresh sardines
½ tablespoon salt
4 limes
1 green chilli
100 g (3½ oz) fresh coriander leaves, chopped roughly

❶ Prepare and pre-heat the barbecue for grilling (page 6).
❷ Clean the fish by cutting them open along the belly from just below the head to the tail. Scrape away the insides with a knife.
❸ Rinse the fish well under cold running water. Pat dry with kitchen paper. Sprinkle the insides with the salt.
❹ Grate the zest from one lime and squeeze its juice into a small bowl. Cut a second lime into thin slices and reserve. Cut the chilli in thin slices. Combine the lime juice, lime zest and sliced chilli.
❺ Lightly slash both sides of each fish in 3 or 4 places. Rub the lime and chilli mixture inside and over each fish.
❻ Place the fish in a shallow dish. Scatter the coriander over the fish. Place the reserved lime slices over the coriander and refrigerate for one hour.
❼ Brush oil over the inside of the broiler, both sides of the fish and on the grill bars.
❽ Discard the lime slices and place the fish in the broiler. Grill each side for 3–4 minutes. If no broiler is available, use a pair of long metal skewers to impale several fish at once. Impale the first skewer just below the head and the second skewer just above the tail. Alternate the sardines head to tail on the parallel skewers and cook on a well-oiled grill for 3–4 minutes on each side. Baste with oil frequently during cooking.
❾ Serve with fresh lime wedges, cut from 2 remaining limes.

Grilled Herring with Apple and Cheese Stuffing

Preparation time: 15 minutes + 10–20 minutes cooking. Freezing: not recommended. Serves 4.

A delicately flavoured fish which is at its shiny fresh best for summer barbecues.

4 fresh herrings, cleaned
50 g (2 oz) butter or margarine
1 small onion, chopped finely
1 dessert apple, grated coarsely
50 g (2 oz) Cheddar cheese, grated
25 g (1 oz) fresh breadcrumbs
grated zest of ½ orange
4 tablespoons orange juice
salt and pepper
orange wedges and parsley, to garnish
8 wooden cocktail sticks, soaked in water

❶ Prepare and pre-heat the barbecue for grilling (page 6).
❷ Scrape the herrings to remove all the scales. Discard the heads and trim the tails. Make three diagonal cuts across each side of the fish.
❸ Melt 25 g (1 oz) of the butter in a small saucepan. Add the onion and cook until it softens and becomes translucent.
❹ Stir the apple, cheese, breadcrumbs and orange zest into the saucepan and season well with salt and pepper. Cool slightly.
❺ Stuff each fish with the apple and cheese mixture and secure the slits with well-wetted wooden cocktail sticks.
❻ Melt the remaining butter in a small saucepan and stir in the orange juice.
❼ Place the herrings directly on to a well-oiled grill or into an oiled broiler and cook over a medium-high heat for 5–8 minutes on each side until the skin is crisp and the flesh flakes easily. Baste frequently with the orange-butter during grilling.
❽ Remove the cocktail sticks and serve the stuffed herring with a garnish of orange wedges and parsley.

Lime-seasoned Salmon Steaks with Herb and Crème Fraîche Sauce

Preparation time: 10 minutes + 1 hour marinating + 10 minutes cooking.
Freezing: not recommended. Serves 4.

This is a real treat for a fish-lover; the rich taste of salmon with a tangy accent, topped off with a luxurious aromatic sauce.

4 × 125–150 g (4–5 oz) salmon steaks

For the marinade:

3 tablespoons oil
3 tablespoons fresh lime juice
2 tablespoons water
1 tablespoon soy sauce
¼ teaspoon dill weed

For the sauce:

1 garlic clove, chopped finely
1 tablespoon chopped fresh basil
1 teaspoon tarragon leaves
½ teaspoon marjoram leaves
200 ml (7 fl oz) carton crème fraîche
salt and pepper
parsley, to garnish

❶ Prepare and pre-heat the barbecue for grilling (page 6).
❷ Combine the marinade ingredients in a bowl and mix well.
❸ Wipe the steaks with a damp cloth and place them in a plastic bag, set in a shallow dish. Pour the marinade over the fish and tightly seal the bag. Refrigerate for 1 hour, occasionally turning over the bag to distribute the marinade evenly.
❹ Meanwhile, mix together the sauce ingredients. Season to taste with salt and pepper and cover.
❺ Liberally oil the grill. If using a hinged broiler, brush oil over the inside of the broiler, both sides of the fish and on the grill bars. Grill over a medium-high heat for 5–6 minutes on each side.
❻ Transfer the fish to a warm serving dish and garnish with sprigs of parsley. Serve immediately with the sauce.

Caraway Mackerel with Lemon Sauce

Preparation time: 15 minutes + 30 minutes marinating + 12–15 minutes cooking.
Freezing: not recommended. Serves 4.

Mackerel is a firm fish, ideal for barbecuing. Its rich, savoury flavour is nicely complemented by the tangy lemon sauce.

4 × 250 g (8 oz) fresh mackerel
2 tablespoons sunflower oil
½ teaspoon garlic salt
½ teaspoon pepper
1 teaspoon caraway seeds
For the lemon basting sauce:
175 g (6 oz) butter
1 teaspoon sugar
1 teaspoon salt
2 teaspoons paprika
½ teaspoon pepper
¼ teaspoon mustard powder
125 ml (4 fl oz) lemon juice
125 ml (4 fl oz) hot water

❶ Prepare and pre-heat the barbecue for grilling (page 6).
❷ Clean the mackerel and, if desired, discard the heads. Rinse well under cold running water. Pat dry with kitchen paper.
❸ Slash each side of the fish diagonally with 3 or 4 cuts, about 5 mm (¼ inch) deep. Place the fish, head to tail, in a shallow glass dish. Mix the oil, garlic salt, pepper and caraway seeds and brush over the fish. Cover the dish and refrigerate for 30 minutes.
❹ Melt the butter in a small saucepan and stir in the sugar, salt, paprika, pepper and mustard powder. Blend in the lemon juice and hot water.
❺ Place the mackerel directly on to a well-oiled grill or into a well-oiled broiler and cook over a medium-high heat for 5–8 minutes on each side, basting frequently with the lemon sauce.

Tuna Steaks with Herb Butter

Preparation time: 10 minutes + 1 hour standing + 10–12 minutes cooking.
Freezing: not recommended. Serves 4.

The herb butter can be made up to seven days before you use it, providing it is kept in a covered dish in the refrigerator.

4 tuna steaks, 2–2.5 cm (¾–1 inch) thick
90 ml (3 fl oz) olive oil
1 teaspoon paprika
2 tablespoons white wine vinegar
a pinch of salt
For the herb butter:
4 tablespoons unsalted butter, softened
1 tablespoon finely chopped fresh herbs (use mild herbs such as parsley, thyme and chervil, either separately or in combination)
1 teaspoon very finely chopped shallot or onion
grated zest of ¼ lemon
salt, pepper and lemon juice

❶ Prepare and pre-heat the barbecue for grilling (page 6).
❷ Place the tuna steaks in a shallow glass dish. Combine the oil, paprika, vinegar and salt and pour over the fish, turning to coat well. Cover the dish and refrigerate for about 1 hour and then let it stand at room temperature for 30 minutes more.
❸ Beat the butter until soft. Mix in the herbs, shallot or onion and lemon zest. Taste and adjust the seasoning, using the salt, pepper and lemon juice. Set aside for 1 hour for the flavours to blend.
❹ Place the tuna steaks on a well-oiled grill, or into a well-oiled broiler and cook over a medium-high heat for 5–6 minutes on each side, basting continuously with the marinade.
❺ Serve immediately with a tablespoon of the herb butter on top of each steak.

Meat

For many people nothing conjures up 'barbecuing' as does the image of meat sizzling away on the grill. The handsome, 'tram-lined' exterior of the meat promises a juicy and succulent meal. As with fish, the grilling time of meat is regulated by its thickness. In the case of beef, as a rule of thumb, allow roughly 8–10 minutes for each 2.5 cm (1-inch) thickness for a rare steak, 12 minutes for a medium steak and 16–20 minutes for a well-done steak. Fillet, rib, rump, T-bone, porterhouse and, of course, sirloin are the cuts which provide the tenderest steaks, but tougher cuts can be tenderised in marinades and grilled quite satisfactorily.

Minced meats such as hamburger should be cooked through until the centre is piping hot and no pink colour remains.

Florida-style Lamb Cutlets

Preparation time: 5 minutes + minimum of 4 hours marinating + 15 minutes cooking.
Freezing: not recommended. Serves 6.

Lamb cutlets are simplicity itself to cook on the barbecue. This subtly spiced, citrus-based marinade makes them something quite special.

12 best-end lamb cutlets

For the marinade:

6 tablespoons orange juice

3 tablespoons sunflower oil

1 tablespoon brown sugar

1½ teaspoons ground cinnamon

¼ teaspoon pepper

¼ teaspoon salt

❶ Place the cutlets in a single layer in a shallow dish.

❷ Combine the marinade ingredients. Reserve 2–3 tablespoons and pour the rest over the cutlets. Turn until the cutlets are evenly coated. Leave them to marinate at room temperature for about 4 hours or overnight in the refrigerator.

❸ Prepare and pre-heat the barbecue for grilling (page 6).

❹ Drain the cutlets and cook over a medium heat for about 15 minutes, turning occasionally. Baste frequently with the reserved marinade during cooking.

Spit-roasted Chilli-stuffed Leg of Lamb

Preparation time: 15 minutes + 1–2 hours cooking. Freezing: recommended after step 4. Serves 8.

Rôtisserie cooking is one of the most sociable ways of barbecuing. As the rôtisserie is doing the work, the cook is free to relax with his or her guests. If you don't have a rôtisserie spit, you can roast the lamb in a covered barbecue, allowing approximately 22–25 minutes of cooking per pound of meat.

2.75 kg (6 lb) leg of lamb, boned
50 g (2 oz) butter, melted
For the stuffing:
1 green pepper, chopped finely
3 onions, chopped finely
3 garlic cloves, chopped finely
2 small dried red chilli peppers
2 teaspoons ground cumin
½ teaspoon salt
¼ teaspoon pepper

❶ Prepare and pre-heat the barbecue for spit-roasting (page 6).
❷ Combine the stuffing ingredients and grind them into a paste (a mortar and pestle is ideal for this task but you can use a food processor if you prefer).
❸ Spread the paste evenly over the inside of the boned leg of lamb.
❹ Roll up the meat as tightly as possible, from its narrowest point to its widest edge, and tie it securely with fine string every 2.5 cm (1 inch) along the length of the roll.
❺ Position the meat on the spit, testing it for balance by rotating the ends of the spit slowly. If there is no tendency for the meat to roll suddenly from any position, the balance is adequate for even rotation. If the meat does roll unevenly, re-skewer it to correct the imbalance.
❻ Put the spit on the barbecue and turn on the spit motor, again checking that the meat turns evenly. Cook for about 1–2 hours, occasionally basting the meat with the melted butter during the first 30 minutes of cooking. The lamb is ready when a meat thermometer pushed into the centre of its thickest part shows the required temperature: 60°C (140°F) for rare meat; 71°C (160°F) for medium; and 77°C (170°F) for well-done meat.
❼ Leave the cooked lamb for 10–15 minutes before carving it into slices.

Rancho Burgers

Preparation time: 15 minutes + 20 minutes cooking. Freezing: recommended after step 4. Serves 6.

A classic burger recipe which smells as good as it tastes! For an extra boost of flavour, melt a slice of strong Cheddar cheese on top during the last few minutes of grilling.

1 small onion, chopped finely
1 green pepper, chopped finely
2 carrots, grated
1 garlic clove, crushed
500 g (1 lb) chuck steak, minced finely
2 teaspoons Worcestershire sauce
1 tablespoon oil
50 g (2 oz) soft white breadcrumbs
¼ teaspoon salt
¼ teaspoon pepper
1 egg, beaten lightly
To serve:
6 soft rolls, halved
2 large tomatoes, sliced

❶ Prepare and pre-heat the barbecue for grilling (page 6).
❷ Sauté the onion, green pepper, carrots and garlic until softened, and drain well on 2–3 sheets of kitchen paper.
❸ In a large bowl, lightly but thoroughly mix together the sautéed vegetables with the minced steak, Worcestershire sauce, oil, breadcrumbs and salt and pepper. Bind together the mixture with the beaten egg.
❹ Shape the mixture into 6 patties and drain, if necessary, on 2–3 sheets of kitchen paper.
❺ Cook on an oiled grill over a medium-high heat for approximately 20 minutes, turning once.
❻ Ensure the burgers are cooked through, the centres are piping hot and no pink colour remains.
❼ During the final few minutes of cooking, toast the rolls on the barbecue grill.
❽ Garnish each burger with tomato slices and serve immediately in the rolls.

Sausage, Bacon and Mushroom Kebabs

Preparation time: 15 minutes + 15 minutes cooking. Freezing: not recommended. Serves 2 (makes 4 kebabs).

This recipe can be varied by using any herby sausage. Extra vegetables such as peppers, shallots and parboiled new potatoes may be added.

6 × 50 g (2 oz) Lincolnshire pork sausages
4 rashers streaky bacon, rind removed
8 button mushrooms

For the baste:
2 tablespoons tomato paste
2 teaspoons Worcestershire sauce
1 teaspoon clear honey
1 tablespoon corn oil

❶ Prepare and pre-heat the barbecue for grilling (page 6).
❷ Combine the ingredients for the baste in a saucepan and heat gently until well blended. Place to one side of the grill.
❸ Twist each sausage in its middle and cut to form two stubby links.
❹ Stretch each bacon rasher with the back of a knife, cut in half and roll up.
❺ Lightly oil four metal skewers and thread each with 2 bacon rolls, 3 small sausages and 2 button mushrooms alternately.
❻ Brush the baste over the kebabs and place them on a lightly-oiled grill. Cook over a medium-high heat for about 15 minutes, brushing them with more baste and turning during cooking.

Beef Kebabs with Garlic Baste

Preparation time: 15 minutes + 8–10 minutes cooking. Freezing: not recommended. Serves 4.

As an alternative try using green peppers and mushrooms.

1 kg (2 lb) rump, sirloin or fillet steak, trimmed and cut into 2.5 cm (1-inch) cubes
2 courgettes, sliced into 2 cm (¾-inch) pieces.
4 firm ripe tomatoes, quartered

For the garlic baste:
3 tablespoons groundnut oil
3 tablespoons soft butter
1 garlic clove, crushed
¼ teaspoon pepper

❶ Prepare and pre-heat the barbecue for grilling (page 6).
❷ Place the oil, butter, garlic and pepper in a small saucepan and heat gently for a few minutes until the butter is melted. Keep the pan to one side of the grill.
❸ Thread the meat cubes, courgette slices and tomato segments alternately on to metal skewers (preferably flat-bladed). Brush the kebabs with the garlic baste.
❹ Grill over a medium-high heat, turning and basting frequently, for about 10 minutes. Make sure the meat is cooked through until the centre is piping hot and no pink colour remains.

Spicy Citrus and Honey-Glazed Spare-ribs

Preparation time: 15 minutes + 12–24 hours marinating + 1¼ hours cooking.
Freezing: not recommended. Serves 4.

Eating pork spare-ribs requires (and always gets) tremendous concentration to ensure that every last morsel is stripped from the bone. There are many mouth-watering spare-rib recipes, but this one is particularly moreish.

1.25 kg (3 lb) meaty spare-ribs, cut into individual rib sections
For the marinade and glaze:
2 tablespoons clear honey
juice of ½ lemon
grated zest and juice of ½ orange
2 tablespoons Worcestershire sauce
2 teaspoons soy sauce
salt

❶ Combine the marinade ingredients in a small saucepan and heat gently. Simmer for 5 minutes and allow the marinade to cool.
❷ Place a large plastic bag in a large roasting tin and put the ribs in the bag. Pour in the marinade and seal the bag with a twist-tie. Refrigerate for 12–24 hours, turning the bag occasionally.
❸ Pre-heat the oven to Gas Mark 4/180°C/350°F. Briefly drain the spare-ribs, reserving the marinade, and place them in the roasting tin.
❹ Roast the spare-ribs in the oven for 1 hour. Alternatively, you can use a covered barbecue to part-cook the ribs, using the roasting or baking technique (page 8).
❺ Meanwhile, prepare and pre-heat the barbecue for grilling (page 6).
❻ Remove the spare-ribs from the roasting tin. Drain and place them on a lightly-oiled grill. Cook for about 12–15 minutes, turning and basting continuously, until the meat has pulled away about 1 cm (½ inch) from the end of the rib bone.

Poultry

Chicken, turkey, duck, goose, guinea fowl or quail – in fact any poultry does seem to taste better, look better and gain in succulence for having been grilled, roasted, spit-roasted or smoke-cooked on a barbecue.

It is particularly important for food-safety reasons that poultry is cooked right through. If you like, you can part-cook poultry in the microwave before barbecuing. If you have one, use a microwave roasting rack to prevent the meat from cooking in its juices. Remember also to drain off the marinade before microwaving and do not baste the meat until it is on the barbecue. When the thickest part of the meat is pierced with a fork or skewer, its juices should run clear and not pink.

'Cheese and Streaky' Stuffed Drumsticks

Preparation time: 15 minutes + 25–30 minutes cooking. Freezing: not recommended. Serves 4.

For a bigger and equally tasty mouthful, turkey drumsticks can be substituted for chicken. Adjust the cooking time according to the weight and thickness of the turkey drumsticks (some of which can be as big as a small leg of lamb).

8 chicken drumsticks
75 g (3 oz) cream cheese
8 rashers streaky bacon
sunflower oil or melted butter, for basting
salt and pepper
8 wooden cocktail sticks (well soaked in water)

❶ Prepare and pre-heat the barbecue for grilling (page 6).

❷ Using a sharp short-bladed knife, make a deep incision in the thickest part of each drumstick and pack the slit with cream cheese.

❸ Season to taste with salt and pepper and wrap a rasher of bacon tightly around each drumstick. Secure the bacon with cocktail sticks.

❹ Place the prepared drumsticks on a lightly-oiled grill and cook over a medium-high heat for about 12–15 minutes on each side, basting frequently with the oil or melted butter. Make sure that, when pierced with a fork, the juices run clear and no pink colour remains.

Tandoori Chicken

Preparation time: 30 minutes + 4–12 hours marinating + 30–40 minutes cooking.
Freezing: recommended after step 3. Serves 4–6.

This particular recipe uses chicken portions, but if you own a covered barbecue you can try using it as a surrogate tandoor (clay oven) to cook a whole bird. Simply set up your covered barbecue for roasting (page 6) and prepare the chicken and Tandoori marinade as described below. Allow about 1 hour to roast a chicken weighing 1.25 kg (3 lb), or cook until the juices run clear when the inside of the chicken thigh is pierced with a skewer. Bottled Tandoori paste is readily available at supermarkets and is a fine substitute if you don't have time to make your own.

2 × 1 kg (2 lb) fresh chicken, quartered
juice of 1½ lemons
melted ghee or vegetable oil for brushing
For the Tandoori marinade:
4 garlic cloves
1 cm (½-inch) piece of fresh root ginger, peeled and chopped finely or ½ teaspoon of freeze-dried ginger
1 teaspoon roasted cumin seeds, ground or 1 teaspoon ground cumin
½ teaspoon ground cardamom
½ teaspoon ground cinnamon
¼ teaspoon ground nutmeg
1 teaspoon chilli powder
1 teaspoon salt
125 g (4 oz) natural yogurt
lemon wedges, to serve

❶ Using kitchen paper (for a better grip) pull the skin off the chicken pieces. Pierce the meat several times with the point of a skewer or a sharp kitchen fork. Make deep diagonal cuts in the meat about 2.5 cm (1 inch) apart.
❷ Place the chicken portions in a large bowl. Sprinkle with the lemon juice and rub in well for a minute or two. Cover the bowl and refrigerate for 30 minutes.
❸ Combine the marinade ingredients in a food processor or blender and blend until the mixture is smooth. Pour the marinade over the chicken portions and mix thoroughly to coat. Cover the bowl and refrigerate for at least 4 hours or overnight. Remove the marinated chicken from the refrigerator 1–2 hours before cooking.
❹ Prepare and pre-heat the barbecue for grilling (page 6).
❺ Place the chicken, bone side down, on a lightly-oiled grill and brush the cut surface of the meat with melted ghee or oil. Cook over a medium-high heat for 10 minutes. Turn and baste the other side and cook for 10 minutes more. Continue to cook, turning and basting every 10 minutes or so, until the meat is done – this will take 30–40 minutes. Make sure that, when pierced with a fork, the juices run clear and no pink colour remains. Serve the chicken with lemon wedges and a salad.

Coriander and Ginger Kebabs

Preparation time: 15 minutes + 4–12 hours marinating + 10–15 minutes cooking.
Freezing: not recommended. Serves 4.

Chicken breast is always popular and this is one of the most delicious ways to cook it, making it spicy, tangy and very succulent.

500 g (1 lb) boneless chicken breasts or thighs, skinned
For the marinade:
1 garlic clove, crushed
½ teaspoon freeze-dried ginger or ground ginger
½ teaspoon ground coriander
3 tablespoons clear honey
2 tablespoons olive oil
2 tablespoons dry vermouth or dry white wine
2 tablespoons soy sauce
juice of ½ lime

❶ Mix the marinade ingredients together in a large shallow dish.
❷ Cut the chicken into 2.5 cm (1-inch) cubes and put the cubes in the marinade. Cover and refrigerate the dish for at least 4 hours, or overnight, and remove from the refrigerator 1 hour before cooking.
❸ Prepare and pre-heat the barbecue for grilling (page 6).
❹ Reserve the marinade and thread the chicken cubes on to oiled metal skewers (preferably flat-bladed) and cook them over a medium heat for 10–15 minutes, turning frequently. Baste the kebabs with the marinade towards the end of cooking. Do not cook over excessive heat as the meat will become dry, but before serving make sure that, when pierced with a fork, the juices run clear and no pink colour remains.

Devilled Drumsticks

Preparation time: 10 minutes + 30 minutes cooking.
Freezing: not recommended. Serves 4.

Drumsticks are the perfect finger-food – give them a spicy, piquant baste like this one and your guests just won't be able to resist.

8 chicken drumsticks
For the baste:
4 tablespoons butter, melted
1 teaspoon chilli powder
2 garlic cloves, chopped very finely
2 tablespoons lime juice
½ teaspoon grated lime zest
¼ teaspoon ground cumin

❶ Prepare and pre-heat the barbecue for grilling (page 6).
❷ Mix together the ingredients for the baste and generously brush the drumsticks with the mixture.
❸ Place the drumsticks on a lightly-oiled grill and cook over a medium-high heat for about 30 minutes or until the juices run clear when the thickest part of the meat is pierced with a skewer. Turn and baste the chicken frequently while cooking.

Cranberry Glazed Chicken Wings

Preparation time: 15 minutes + 1–2 hours marinating + 15–20 minutes cooking.
Freezing: not recommended. Makes 32.

These very tasty wings make excellent appetisers although they are so moreish that many people may not want to wait for the main course!

16 chicken wings, cut into individual joints with the tips removed

For the marinade:

3 tablespoons sunflower oil

3 tablespoons lemon juice

1 tablespoon soy sauce

½ teaspoon seasoned pepper

For the glaze:

90 ml (3 fl oz) cranberry sauce

3 tablespoons clear honey

grated zest of 1 orange

❶ Place the chicken wings in a large dish. Combine the oil, lemon juice, soy sauce and pepper and pour over the chicken pieces, mixing thoroughly to coat. Refrigerate for 1–2 hours.

❷ Prepare and pre-heat the barbecue for grilling (page 6).

❸ Reserving the marinade, drain the chicken wings and place them on a lightly-oiled grill. Cook for 10 minutes over a medium-high heat, turning several times.

❹ Meanwhile, stir the cranberry sauce, honey and orange zest into the remaining marinade and brush generously over the chicken. Continue to cook for a further 5–10 minutes until the skin of the chicken is richly glazed and until the juices run clear when the thickest part of the wing is pierced with a fork or skewer.

Hickory-smoked Turkey with Scottish Glaze

Preparation time: 10 minutes + 2–2¾ hours cooking. Freezing: not recommended. Serves 12–14.

A smoke-cooked barbecued turkey provides a wonderful sight and smell. Why not forgo the kitchen oven this Christmas and roast the family turkey al fresco? Not only will you end up with a delicious dinner, but you'll save on both oven space and washing up!

4.5–6 kg (10–14 lb) turkey
3 tablespoons groundnut oil
½ teaspoon salt
¼ teaspoon pepper
2–3 handfuls of hickory chips, well soaked in water

For the glaze:
75 g (3 oz) melted butter
3 tablespoons Drambuie
1 teaspoon clear honey

❶ Prepare and pre-heat the barbecue for roasting (page 6).
❷ Rinse the turkey inside and out under cold running water. Pat dry with kitchen paper.
❸ Twist the wings under the back or fasten them next to the breast by tying them securely across the bird's body. Tie the legs together at the knuckles, allowing them to lie slightly open in order to let the heat reach the crevice where the legs join the body. Cover the wing tips and the ends of the legs (from the knuckle to half-way up the calf muscle) with foil.
❹ Brush the bird's surface with the oil and lightly season it inside and out with salt and pepper.
❺ Place the bird, breast side up, in the centre of the grill, directly over the drip pan. Slip a 10 cm (4-inch) wide band of kitchen foil under the turkey where it sits on the grill. This will prevent the bird's underside from becoming charred.
❻ Cook with the lid down for 2–2¾ hours: after 30 minutes of cooking, scatter 2 handfuls of well-soaked hickory chips on the charcoal fire-bed or directly on the gas barbecue's volcanic rock/ceramic briquettes or metal heat-plate. Repeat with another handful of chips about 30 minutes before the bird is ready. The bird is done when a meat thermometer registers 82°C (180°F) or when the juices run clear when the inside of the bird's thigh is pierced with a skewer.
❼ Meanwhile, combine the butter and honey in a small saucepan and gently heat through before adding the Drambuie. Brush this glaze over the turkey during the final 30 minutes of cooking.
❽ Remove the turkey from the barbecue and allow to stand for 15–20 minutes before carving.

Note: Should you prefer your turkey to have a light golden hue rather than a dark mahogany colour, cover the bird with a sheet of foil for 30–40 minutes during the middle of cooking. Alternatively, omit or reduce the second application of hickory chips.

Spit-roasted Duck with Tangy Soy Sauce

Preparation time: 15 minutes + 1½–2 hours cooking. Freezing: not recommended. Serves 4.

Allow between 375 g (12 oz) and 500 g (1 lb) of uncooked duck per person. Most of us who have ever eaten in a Chinese restaurant have fond memories of succulent duck, with crispy skin and a subtle Oriental flavour. This version is every bit as good with the added bonus of the aroma and tang that only barbecuing can give.

2 kg (4½ lb) duck
½ teaspoon thyme (lemon-scented if available)
1 teaspoon salt
For the glaze:
3 tablespoons soy sauce
90 ml (3 fl oz) orange juice
1½ tablespoons clear honey
¼ teaspoon pepper
For the tangy soy sauce:
90 ml (3 fl oz) orange juice
4 tablespoons soy sauce
125 ml (4 fl oz) dry white wine
3 tablespoons water
6 tablespoons brown sugar
2 dashes Tabasco sauce
1 shallot, chopped finely
½ teaspoon mustard powder
½ teaspoon paprika
a large pinch of ground cinnamon
2 teaspoons cornflour, made into a paste with a little water
salt and pepper

❶ Prepare and pre-heat the barbecue for spit-roasting (page 6).

❷ Remove the giblets from the duck and cut off and discard its wing-tips and excess fat. Rinse the duck under cold running water and pat dry with kitchen paper. Pierce the meat in several places with a skewer or sharp pointed fork and sprinkle the cavity with the thyme and 1 teaspoon of salt.

❸ Truss the duck as compactly as possible. Push the spit in just in front of the tail – 'parson's nose' – through to a point near the apex of the wish-bone (the spit should run diagonally through the cavity of the duck). Tightly secure the meat tines at either end of the bird.

❹ Combine the soy sauce, orange juice, honey and pepper in a small saucepan and warm through.

❺ Cook the duck for 1½–2 hours or until the skin is crisp and golden brown and the juices run clear when the meat is pierced with a skewer. Brush the warm glaze over the duck two or three times during the first hour of cooking and again two or three times during the final 25 minutes.

❻ Meanwhile, combine in a saucepan all of the ingredients for the sauce except for the cornflour paste and salt and pepper. Bring them slowly to a boil, stirring constantly. Simmer for 5–6 minutes then add the cornflour paste and stir until thickened. Season with the salt and pepper and serve with the duck.

P

Vegetarian

Barbecuing without meat may seem odd to some, but, in addition to the wide variety of vegetables which can be cooked directly on the grill – aubergines, mushrooms, onions, courgettes and tomatoes – there are many others which are delicious when dotted with seasoned butter and wrapped in foil before cooking. Try a mixture of sliced carrots and peas, sprinkled with fresh chopped mint.

Meat substitutes such as Quorn and tofu can be made into tasty burgers or kebabs. As both products absorb flavours well, experiment with bastes and sauces until you find your favourite!

Grilled Halloumi with Lemon and Garlic Vinaigrette

Preparation time: 5 minutes + 2–3 minutes cooking. Freezing: not recommended. Serves 4 as a starter.

This makes a very tasty appetiser with great eye appeal. Halloumi (which originates from Cyprus) is sold in block form. Stored in its own brine, in sealed packs, it will keep for 5–6 days in a refrigerator after the pack is opened, providing it remains in its brine. In order to bring an extra dash of Mediterranean sunshine to the vinaigrette, lemon juice has been substituted for the usual wine vinegar.

1 Halloumi cheese

For the lemon and garlic vinaigrette dressing:

1 tablespoon lemon juice

1 garlic clove, chopped very finely

¼ teaspoon pepper

1 rounded teaspoon mustard powder

1 tablespoon chopped fresh coriander leaves

3 tablespoons extra virgin olive oil

❶ Prepare and pre-heat the barbecue for grilling (page 6).

❷ Unwrap the cheese, rinse under cold running water and pat dry with kitchen paper. Cut the block in 8 even slices.

❸ Place the vinaigrette ingredients in a small bowl and whisk together until thoroughly blended. If making the vinaigrette well beforehand, store it in a screw-top jar and shake vigorously just before using.

❹ Place the cheese slices on to an oiled grill and cook over medium-high heat for about 1 minute on each side or until the Halloumi is a light golden colour. Do not overcook. Unlike the softer Greek cheeses, Halloumi becomes tough and chewy when cooked too long.

❺ Cut in strips and serve immediately, on warm plates, sprinkled with the vinaigrette.

Greek-style Quorn Kebabs with Minty Yogurt Sauce

Preparation time: 15 minutes + 1 hour standing + 10–12 minutes cooking.
Freezing: not recommended. Serves 4.

Simple but delicious, this nutritious adaptation of a favourite Greek dish is ideal for barbecuing. Quorn is low in fat and cholesterol-free so your guests won't feel guilty coming back for seconds!

- 1 egg, beaten
- 2 tablespoons plain yogurt
- 40 g (1½ oz) dried white breadcrumbs
- 25 g (1 oz) finely chopped onion
- 1 tablespoon finely chopped parsley
- 2 teaspoons chopped fresh oregano or ½ teaspoon dried oregano, crushed
- ¼ teaspoon salt
- a pinch of pepper
- 375 g (12 oz) diced Quorn
- olive oil

For the sauce:

- 150 g (5 oz) plain yogurt
- 25 g (1 oz) cucumber, peeled, de-seeded and chopped finely
- 2 teaspoons chopped fresh mint or ½ teaspoon dried mint leaves, crushed
- 1 teaspoon chopped fresh dill or ¼ teaspoon dried dill weed

To serve:

- 2 pitta breads, wrapped in foil
- shredded lettuce

❶ Mix together the ingredients for the sauce in a small bowl. Cover and refrigerate for at least 1 hour to allow the flavours to blend.

❷ Prepare and pre-heat the barbecue for grilling (page 6).

❸ Combine the beaten egg and the yogurt in a mixing bowl. Stir in the breadcrumbs, onion, parsley, oregano, salt and pepper. Add the Quorn and mix until all the ingredients are thoroughly combined. Refrigerate for 30 minutes or until the mixture is firm to the touch.

❹ Brush the skewers (preferably flat-bladed) with olive oil.

❺ Divide the chilled Quorn mixture in 4 parts and, using wet hands, shape into 4 sausage-shaped kebabs. Press each kebab on to a skewer, tapering the ends to leave no gap between the kebabs and the skewer blades.

❻ Brush the kebabs with oil and place them on a well-oiled grill with the skewer handles facing towards you, away from the radiant heat. Grill over a medium-high heat for 5–6 minutes each side, until the centre is piping hot.

❼ During the last few minutes of cooking, heat the foil-wrapped bread on the edge of the grill. Halve the pittas across and stuff the pockets with shredded lettuce. Place the skewered kebab inside the pocket, and grasp firmly before withdrawing the skewer.

❽ Spoon the minty yogurt sauce into the pitta pockets and serve immediately.

Mixed Vegetable Kebabs with Herb Butter

Preparation time: 20 minutes + 10 minutes cooking. Freezing: not recommended. Serves 6.

Nothing could be more simple or delicious than grilled vegetables flavoured with a mixture of summer herbs and butter. Experiment with combinations of your own – sweetcorn, courgettes, aubergine – the possibilities are endless!

6 new or small potatoes, scrubbed or peeled thinly
6 small onions, peeled
1 large green pepper, de-seeded and cut in 6
12 closed-cup button mushrooms, wiped and de-stemmed
6 small firm and ripe tomatoes

For the herb butter:
50 g (2 oz) melted butter
1 teaspoon finely chopped fresh tarragon or ½ teaspoon dried tarragon
2 teaspoons finely chopped fresh chives
2 teaspoons finely chopped fresh parsley
½ teaspoon garlic salt
¼ teaspoon pepper

❶ Prepare and pre-heat the barbecue for grilling (page 6).
❷ Cook the potatoes and onions separately in lightly-salted boiling water until barely tender. Drain well.
❸ Thread the potatoes, onions, pepper and mushrooms on to oiled skewers.
❹ Blend the melted butter, tarragon, chives, parsley, garlic salt and pepper together. Brush the kebabs generously with the mixture and place them on a lightly-oiled grill. Cook over a medium-high heat for 5 minutes, turning once. Add a tomato to the end of each skewer and baste the kebabs with more herb butter. Continue cooking for 5 minutes more, occasionally turning and basting.

Tofu Vegi-burger

Preparation time: 15 minutes + 1½–2 hours for draining and squeezing the tofu + 10–12 minutes cooking.
Freezing: not recommended. Makes 8 burgers.

The savoury taste and firm texture of a tofu vegi-burger is reminiscent of a hamburger – so it is no surprise to learn that throughout East Asia, tofu is known as 'meat without bone'. However, unlike meat, tofu contains no cholesterol and is comparatively low in saturated fats and calories, making it an ideal food for the health-conscious barbecue!

900 g (1 lb 13 oz) tofu, drained and squeezed (see below)
90 g (3 oz) carrot, grated coarsely
2 tablespoons minced spring onions
2 tablespoons minced leek
2 tablespoons ground roasted sesame seeds or ground roasted peanuts
¾ teaspoon salt
groundnut oil for deep frying
8 soft rolls, sliced in half
soy sauce, to serve

❶ Prepare and pre-heat the barbecue for grilling (page 6).
❷ Combine the prepared tofu, carrot, spring onion, leek, ground sesame seeds or peanuts and salt in a large bowl. Mix well and then knead the mixture for about 3 minutes (as you would knead bread dough).
❸ When the mixture has a smooth texture and holds together well, moisten your palms with a little oil and shape the mixture into 8 patties, each about 8 cm (3 inches) in diameter.
❹ Fill a wok, skillet or deep-fryer with about 6 cm (2 inches) of oil and heat it on the barbecue grill to 150°C (300°F). Slide the patties into the hot oil and fry for about 5 minutes on each side or until crisp and golden brown, and the centre is piping hot.
❺ Drain the patties on kitchen paper and serve immediately, sprinkled with soy sauce, in soft rolls.

Preparing the tofu for making patties:
First step: Draining
❶ Wrap the block(s) of tofu firmly in clean cotton cloth or towelling, folded in quarters to create 4 layers of thickness.
❷ Set the wrapped tofu on a plate or shallow dish and refrigerate for 1½ to 2 hours. (This time can be reduced by placing weights on top of the wrapped tofu and exchanging the damp cloth or towelling for dry wrapping after about 30 minutes.)
Note: the tofu is fully drained and ready for squeezing when it can be picked up and held without crumbling.

Second step: Squeezing
❶ Place the drained tofu at the centre of a large, clean dry tea towel. Gather the corners of the towel together.
❷ Twist the tea towel and firmly squeeze the tofu to expel as much water as possible. The tofu is now ready for use.

Bombay Potato Kebabs

Preparation time: 15–20 minutes + 30 minutes marinating + 10 minutes cooking.
Freezing: not recommended. Serves 4.

Potatoes lend themselves surprisingly well to the flavours and spices of the East. This is a simple dish, but quite addictive.

5 tablespoons sunflower oil
1 teaspoon black mustard seeds
1 teaspoon garlic purée
1 onion, chopped finely
3 tablespoons medium-hot curry powder
1 kg (2 lb) potatoes, peeled and cut in 4–5 cm (1½ to 2-inch) cubes
salt

❶ Prepare and pre-heat the barbecue for grilling (page 6).
❷ Heat the oil in a skillet and fry the mustard seeds over a medium heat. Allow the seeds to pop. Have a lid handy to cover the skillet.
❸ Add the garlic purée and onion and fry until the onion is translucent and golden brown. Stir in the curry powder and continue to fry gently for another 2–3 minutes. Remove from heat and set aside.
❹ Parboil the potatoes in lightly salted water for a few minutes or until a skewer can be pushed through with slight pressure (take care not to overcook). Drain thoroughly.
❺ While the cubes are still warm, but not too hot to handle comfortably, thread them on to oiled metal skewers and brush them with the curry paste.
❻ Cover the kebabs and let them stand for about 30 minutes. Cook on an oiled grill over a medium-high heat for about 10 minutes, turning and basting the kebabs with the remaining curry paste from time to time until the potatoes are crisp and nicely coloured.

Vegetables and Salads

Aubergine and Pepper Salad

Preparation time: 10 minutes + 15 minutes cooking. Freezing: not recommended. Serves 4.

A simple but tasty salad originating from Catalonia where a wood fire would have been used instead of a modern barbecue.

2 aubergines
2 red or green peppers
4 tablespoons olive oil
1 garlic clove, chopped finely
3 tablespoons chopped fresh basil
salt

❶ Prepare and pre-heat the barbecue for grilling (page 6).
❷ Lightly oil the grill and cook the aubergines and peppers, turning frequently, for 15 minutes or until the skins are charred and the flesh feels soft.
❸ As soon as they have cooled enough to handle, remove the skins and split them in half lengthwise. Remove the seeds from the peppers and cut both vegetables in long strips. Arrange the strips neatly on a serving dish and season to taste with the olive oil and salt. Sprinkle with the chopped garlic and basil and serve.

Sautéed Courgettes, Green Pepper and Tomatoes

Preparation time: 10 minutes + 20 minutes cooking. Freezing: not recommended. Serves 4–6.

This dish with all the sunny flavours of the Mediterranean would go very well with any grilled meats, especially lamb or chicken.

50 g (2 oz) butter or margarine
2 tablespoons soy sauce
750 g (1½ lb) courgettes, sliced in 2.5 cm (1-inch) rounds
1 green pepper, de-seeded and chopped finely
1 onion, sliced thinly in rings
400 g (13 oz) can of peeled tomatoes, with the juice reserved
a pinch of sugar
pepper

❶ Prepare and pre-heat the barbecue for grilling (page 6).
❷ Melt the butter or margarine in a skillet or heavy baking dish. Stir in the soy sauce.
❸ Add the courgette, pepper and onion rings and sauté over a medium heat until the vegetables are lightly browned.
❹ Add the tomatoes and about half the juice from the can. Season with the sugar and pepper.
❺ Cover the skillet or baking dish with foil and cook for 10 minutes or until the vegetables are just tender, adding more tomato juice if they start to stick.

Waldorf Rice Salad

Preparation and cooking time: 55 minutes. Freezing: not recommended. Serves 6–8.

This is a new version of an old favourite. Unlike some rice salads this is full of flavour and the nuts, celery and apple give it lots of crunch. It would be lovely with spicy grilled meats or fish.

1 tablespoon groundnut oil
300 g (10 oz) brown rice
600 ml (1 pint) boiling water
1 teaspoon salt
2 large tomatoes, cut in thin wedges
½ red or green pepper, de-seeded and chopped finely
1 red dessert apple, cored and chopped roughly
1 small celery stick, chopped finely
2 tablespoons chopped spring onion, or finely chopped onion
25 g (1 oz) walnuts, chopped finely
salt and pepper

For the vinaigrette dressing:

1 garlic clove, crushed
1 teaspoon salt
1 teaspoon mustard powder
1 tablespoon red or white wine vinegar
a pinch of pepper
90 ml (3 fl oz) virgin olive oil
1 tablespoon chopped fresh tarragon (optional)

❶ Heat the oil in a saucepan, add the rice and stir to coat the grains.

❷ Add the boiling water and 1 teaspoon of salt and bring back to a boil. Stir once only, then cover the pan and simmer gently for 40 minutes or until all the liquid has been absorbed and the rice is tender but still slightly firm.

❸ Meanwhile, using a mortar and pestle (or food processor), pound or blend the garlic and salt into a smooth paste.

❹ Add the mustard powder, vinegar and pepper and mix thoroughly until the salt has completely dissolved.

❺ Add the olive oil and tarragon, if using, and pour the vinaigrette into a screw-top jar, giving it a good shake before dressing the salad.

❻ When the rice is ready, turn it into a salad bowl and fluff it with a fork. Pour the dressing over the rice while it is still warm. Allow to cool before folding in the tomatoes, pepper, apple, celery, spring onion (or onion) and chopped walnuts. Season to taste and keep cool until required. If you don't intend to serve the salad within a couple of hours, be sure to keep it in the refrigerator.

Grilled Vegetable Salad with Rocket, Sun-dried Tomatoes and Parmesan Cheese

Preparation time: 20 minutes + 20 minutes cooking
Freezing: not recommended. Serves 4.

This could easily be a meal in itself for a vegetarian. It is absolutely bursting with the smoky flavours of different barbecued vegetables. Toss in some lightly toasted pine kernels if you like.

1 aubergine, cut lengthways in 2 cm (¾-inch) slices
2 fennel bulbs, cut lengthways in thick slices
2 carrots, halved lengthways
1 red pepper, quartered lengthways and de-seeded
1 yellow pepper, quartered lengthways and de-seeded
1 orange pepper, quartered lengthways and de-seeded
1 sweet potato, scrubbed and cut lengthways in thick slices
1 whole garlic bulb (optional)
2 courgettes, cut lengthways in 5 mm (¼-inch) slices
8 spring onions, trimmed at both ends
8 babycorn
1 small cos lettuce
1 handful rocket leaves

For the vinaigrette:
2 tablespoons white wine vinegar
8 tablespoons extra virgin olive oil
1 teaspoon mustard powder
salt and pepper

To garnish:
50 g (2 oz) parmesan cheese
2 sun-dried tomatoes, cut in strips
6 large basil leaves

❶ Prepare and pre-heat the barbecue for grilling (page 6).

❷ Prepare the vinaigrette dressing by placing the ingredients in a screw-top jar and shaking vigorously.

❸ Brush the prepared vegetables (except for the lettuce and rocket) with half the vinaigrette and grill the aubergine, fennel, carrots, peppers, sweet potato and garlic (if using) over a medium-high heat for about 8 minutes.

❹ Turn and baste the vegetables and add the courgettes and spring onions to the grill. Grill for 5 minutes more then turn, adding the babycorn. Brush all the vegetables again with vinaigrette and grill until the corn is just tender. Do not over-cook the vegetables – remove from the grill and keep warm any that are ready before the rest.

❺ Using tongs, remove all the vegetables from the grill. Peel the charred skin from the peppers and remove any charred bits from the other vegetables. Cut the vegetables into bite-sized pieces. Peel the skin from the garlic – the insides will be much milder than when raw.

❻ Arrange the lettuce and rocket in a large salad bowl and toss them thoroughly with the remaining vinaigrette. Scatter the grilled vegetables on to the salad. Use a vegetable peeler to make thin slivers of parmesan cheese. Scatter the slivers of cheese, sun-dried tomatoes and basil leaves over the salad.

Mixed Vegetable Rosti

Preparation time: 25 minutes + 20 minutes cooking.
Freezing: recommended.
Serves 4 as an accompaniment or 2 as a main dish.

This Swiss-inspired potato dish has been given a British flavour by the addition of some favourite root vegetables. Rosti goes well with meat and fish, but this tasty version can easily stand on its own.

2 carrots, scrubbed
2 large baking potatoes, scrubbed and halved
1 orange-fleshed sweet potato, scrubbed
1 celeriac root, scrubbed
1 parsnip, scrubbed
100 g (3½ oz) butter
1 small onion, chopped finely
1 green pepper, chopped finely
salt and pepper
basil, chopped roughly, to garnish

❶ Prepare and pre-heat the barbecue for grilling (page 6).

❷ Place the carrots in a saucepan with water to cover. Boil for about 5 minutes.

❸ Add the potatoes, sweet potato and celeriac to the carrots, plus more water to cover if necessary. Bring back to a boil and cook for 5 minutes more. Add the parsnip and cook for 5 minutes more or until the baking potatoes are just tender (do not overcook).

❹ Drain and cool the vegetables. Thickly peel the celeriac. Peel the other vegetables and grate them coarsely, discarding all the peel.

❺ Melt 3 tablespoons of the butter in a non-stick skillet or frying pan over a medium-high heat. Add the onion and fry until translucent. Stir in the grated carrot, potatoes, sweet potato, celeriac, parsnip and chopped green pepper. Press down lightly with a spatula or fish slice to create a large pancake.

❻ Sprinkle with salt and pepper and dot with 2 tablespoons of butter.

❼ Cook for about 10 minutes or until the underside of the pancake is golden brown. Place a large plate on top of the skillet or pan and carefully invert.

❽ Slip the rosti back into the skillet or pan, dot with 2 more tablespoons of butter and cook for 10 minutes more or until golden brown on both sides.

❾ Remove from the skillet or pan and cut into wedges using a sharp knife or pizza cutter. Sprinkle with the chopped basil and serve immediately.

Fan-Tailed Garlic Roast Potatoes

Preparation time: 15 minutes + 40–50 minutes cooking. Freezing: not recommended. Serves 4.

You'll need a covered barbecue to cook these crusty golden potatoes. Place the roasting tin as close as possible to any meat you may be roasting – this will add to the potatoes' flavour.

4 large evenly-shaped baking potatoes
2 garlic cloves, crushed
125 ml (4 fl oz) groundnut oil
a pinch of paprika
salt

❶ Prepare and pre-heat the barbecue for roasting (page 6).
❷ Slice each potato almost but not quite through at 5 mm (¼-inch) intervals. (Laying the handle of a wooden spoon against the potato's side will prevent the knife from cutting right through it.)
❸ Parboil the cut potatoes for 3 minutes and drain.
❹ Meanwhile, mix the garlic and oil in a small roasting tin and place it in the covered barbecue to heat.
❺ Lay the potatoes, sliced side up, in the pre-heated tin and baste liberally with the hot garlic oil. Sprinkle with salt and the paprika.
❻ Replace the lid of the barbecue and cook for 40–50 minutes, basting occasionally, until the potatoes are tender with a slightly crusty, golden-brown skin.

Orange Butter Glazed Carrots

Preparation time: 25 minutes + 5 minutes cooking. Freezing: not recommended. Serves 4–6.

1 kg (2 lb) carrots, scrubbed and halved if necessary
grated zest and juice of 2 oranges
75 g (3 oz) butter
3 tablespoons brown sugar
salt

❶ Prepare and pre-heat the barbecue for grilling (page 6).
❷ Parboil the carrots in lightly salted water until barely tender and still crisp. Drain well.
❸ Combine the orange zest and juice, butter and sugar in a small saucepan. Heat gently and stir until the sugar has dissolved. Bring the mixture to a boil and simmer gently for 5 minutes.
❹ Dip each carrot in the orange butter sauce, coating them thoroughly. Grill them over a medium heat for 5 minutes, turning and basting occasionally. Any remaining sauce can be re-heated and served with the carrots.

Desserts

It is nice to barbecue an entire meal from start to finish, rather than having to pop indoors to cook dessert in the kitchen. And appetites will be that much keener if your guests can witness the progress of the sweet from the grill to the table.

Grilled Apple Rings

Preparation time: 10 minutes + 6 minutes cooking.
Freezing: not recommended. Serves 4.

Apples and spices were made for each other – a treat to please pretty well everyone.

4 tablespoons brown sugar
1 teaspoon ground cinnamon
½ teaspoon freeze-dried ginger (optional)
50 g (2 oz) melted butter
4 large cooking apples, cored and cut in 2.5 cm (1-inch) slices (with peel intact)
yogurt or crème fraîche, to serve

❶ Prepare and pre-heat the barbecue for grilling (page 6).
❷ Combine the sugar, cinnamon and ginger, if using, with the melted butter.
❸ Brush one side of each apple slice with the spiced butter and place, buttered side down, on a lightly-oiled grill over a medium-high heat. Cook for about 3 minutes.
❹ Generously brush the uncooked side of the apple slices with the spiced butter, turn them over and cook for 3 minutes more, or until the apples feel just tender when prodded with a fork. Serve immediately with yogurt or crème fraîche.

Spicy Barbecued Bananas

Preparation time: 15 minutes + 4–5 minutes cooking. Freezing: not recommended. Serves 4.

A universal favourite with many mouth-watering variations. For children (up to the age of 75), cut a wedge lengthwise along the banana and fill the cavity with a few chocolate chips, some pieces of marshmallow and a sprinkling of raisins. Replace the banana wedge and grill as below. For an all-adult party, you can omit the rum flavouring and substitute a teaspoon or two of a favourite liqueur.

4 medium-ripe firm bananas
juice from 1 lemon
4 pinches of ground cinnamon
4 pinches of ground ginger (optional)
4 teaspoons brown sugar or 2 teaspoons clear honey
1 teaspoon of rum flavouring
4 teaspoons softened butter or margarine
4 pieces heavy-duty foil, approximately 23 × 15 cm (9 × 6 inches)
vanilla ice-cream or whipped cream, to serve

❶ Prepare and pre-heat the barbecue for grilling (page 6).

❷ Peel the bananas and place each in the centre of a piece of foil. Turn the edges of the foil up slightly.

❸ Squeeze or brush lemon juice over each banana and dust them with cinnamon and ginger, if using.

❹ Dribble ½ teaspoon of honey or sprinkle 1 teaspoon of brown sugar over each banana.

❺ Pour ¼ teaspoon of rum flavouring over each banana.

❻ Place a small knob of butter or margarine (about 1 teaspoon) at the base of each banana.

❼ Fold the edges of the foil together, leaving a good gap above the banana. Squeeze together the open ends of the package and turn upwards, so that each resembles a gondola.

❽ Position the foil package on the grill, sealed edges up, over a medium-high heat and cook for about 4 minutes. Open one package and check; if the banana appears to be slightly softening along its base and the butter has fully melted they are ready. Do not overcook as the bananas will become mushy.

❾ Slide the bananas and their sauce on to a plate or serve them in their foil jackets. Serve immediately with vanilla ice-cream or thickly whipped cream.

Mixed Fruit and Bread Kebabs

Preparation time: 10 minutes + 30 minutes marinating + 5–6 minutes cooking.
Freezing: not recommended. Serves 4.

A recipe to try your hand at when summer fruits are plentiful. Keep your eyes open for the exotic and exciting fruits that are now readily available and make up your own version of these tasty dessert kebabs. The toasted caramelised bread cubes are very moreish so you may want to have a few extra on hand!

2 oranges
2 pears, peeled, cored and cut into 2.5 cm (1-inch) cubes
melon balls from 1 small melon
1 small pineapple, peeled, cored and cut into 2.5 cm (1-inch) cubes, or 250 g (8 oz) tin of pineapple chunks
12 large firm strawberries
3 firm bananas, each cut in 4 pieces
juice of 2 lemons
125 g (4 oz) caster sugar, plus extra for dusting
3 tablespoons liqueur of your choice
4 tablespoons white wine
1 large white loaf of bread, crusts removed and cut in 2.5 cm (1-inch) cubes
125 g (4 oz) melted butter

❶ Prepare and pre-heat the barbecue for grilling (page 6).
❷ Cut the unpeeled oranges into 1 cm (½-inch) slices and cut each slice into quarters. Place the orange sections and all the other fruit in a large bowl and add the lemon juice, half the caster sugar and all of the liqueur and wine. Mix very gently and leave in a cool place for 20–30 minutes.
❸ Brush the bread cubes liberally with the melted butter. Toss them in a bowl with the rest of the sugar to coat evenly.
❹ Reserve the marinade and thread the fruit and bread cubes on to long, oiled metal skewers (preferably flat-bladed).
❺ Cook the kebabs over a medium heat, turning and dusting them occasionally with caster sugar, for 5–6 minutes or until they are nicely browned and caramelised. Lightly sprinkle the kebabs with the reserved marinade and serve immediately.

Index

BARBECUES

Garlic and Mustard Grilled Prawns, Bombay Potato Kebabs, Spicy Apple Rings – say goodbye to charred burgers and sausages – barbecuing has never tasted this good!
Barbecues are one of the most relaxing and sociable ways of enjoying food. It seems that few things conjure up the idea of summer quite so readily as the sight and sounds of food sizzling on a grill. Jim Marks's delicious recipes, together with his invaluable advice on barbecues and barbecuing methods, make this the ideal cookbook for both experienced enthusiasts and novices alike.

THE AUTHOR
Jim Marks

Jim Marks, widely regarded as the country's foremost expert on barbecuing, has written several books and makes frequ[illegible]*on the subject.*

0859418766

J Sainsbury plc Stamford House Stamford Street London SE1 9LL
Telephone 0171-921 6000

SAINSBURY'S

Barbecues

40 original recipes with a complete guide to successful barbecuing

Jim Marks